HOW TO DRAW
DINOSAURS

PIXEL
studio

ISBN: 9798342945011

THIS BOOK
belongs to:

_____

LET'S START!

Look at the steps:
Before you start drawing, carefully look at all the steps and decide where you want to place your drawing.

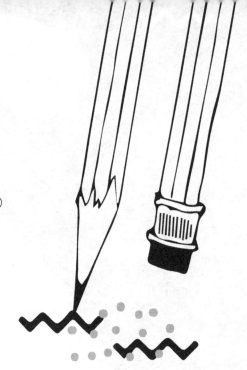

Draw lightly:
Start with light lines, then add stronger ones when you feel more confident.

Don't worry about mistakes:
Don't stress if something doesn't turn out perfectly. Those little mistakes make your drawing unique!

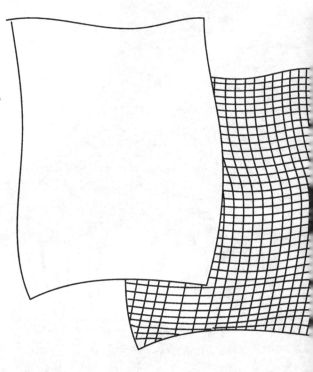

Be creative:
Add more details, take inspiration from the original drawings or come up with your own ideas to make your drawing super interesting.

TOOLS

Prepare a sharp pencil and an eraser:
Start drawing using sharp pencils and an eraser, they allow you to make corrections and not worry when something doesn't go as planned. When you finish drawing, use colorful crayons to bring your dinosaur to life. Crayons are like magical wands that make your dinosaurs look even more beautiful.

Character family:
Once you've learned drawing one object, try drawing a whole family for them, adding different sizes and details. It will be a super fun drawing adventure!

Invite to play:
Also, ask your friends or family to join you in coloring. It's a cool experience where everyone can have their own, magical world of colors!

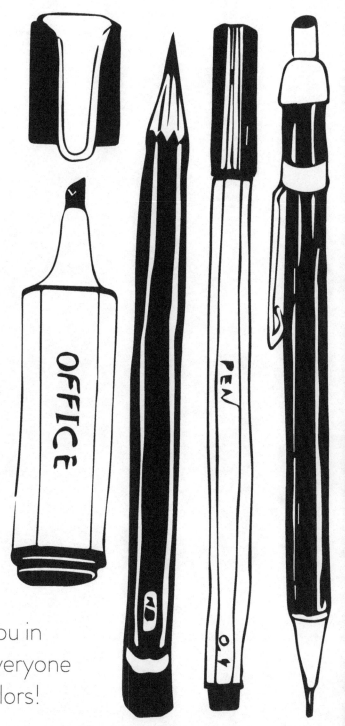

DINOSAURS:

TYRANNOSAURUS REX

WHEN? 68-65 million years ago - in the Late Cretaceous period.

SPEED Up to 20 mph.

SIZE Lenght up to 40 feet.

DIET Carnivorous.

Its name means tyrant lizard king. It is one of the most iconic and feared dinosaurs that ever existed. This gigantic carnivore, which lived during the late Cretaceous period, was known for its colossal size, immense strength, and unparalleled predatory skills. Over the years, it has become a cultural icon and a subject of great scientific interest.

1.

Draw a squarish shape
for the head.

2.

Add an eye, nostrils,
and a large mouth.

3.

Draw a downward curved line
for the back.

4.

Add a line for the belly
and lots of sharp teeth.

5.

Draw two lines for the legs.

6.

Add two more parallel lines
to make the legs thicker.

7.

Finish the legs and draw small arms.

8.

Add details as you like, some color,
and it's done!

TRICERATOPS

WEIGHT

 26,000 pounds.

SIZE

 Hight: 10 feet; Lenght: 30 feet.
Skull lenght: 6.5 feet; Horn lenght 3 feet.

FOOD

  Herbivorous.

Despite its herbivorous diet, the Triceratops was not a passive being. Many Triceratops fossils show bone damage, evidence of fights with rivals and attacks from predators. Its three horns, two above the eyes and one on the snout, were not only defensive weapons but could also have been used in confrontations with other Triceratops over territory or mates. The solid neck frill, made of sturdy bone, provided additional protection against the fierce bites of predators like the Tyrannosaurus rex, and may also have helped regulate its body temperature.

1.

Start with a bean-shaped form –
this will be the head.

2.

Add a frilly collar to the head.

3.

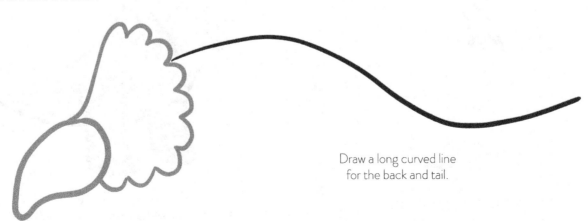

Draw a long curved line
for the back and tail.

4.

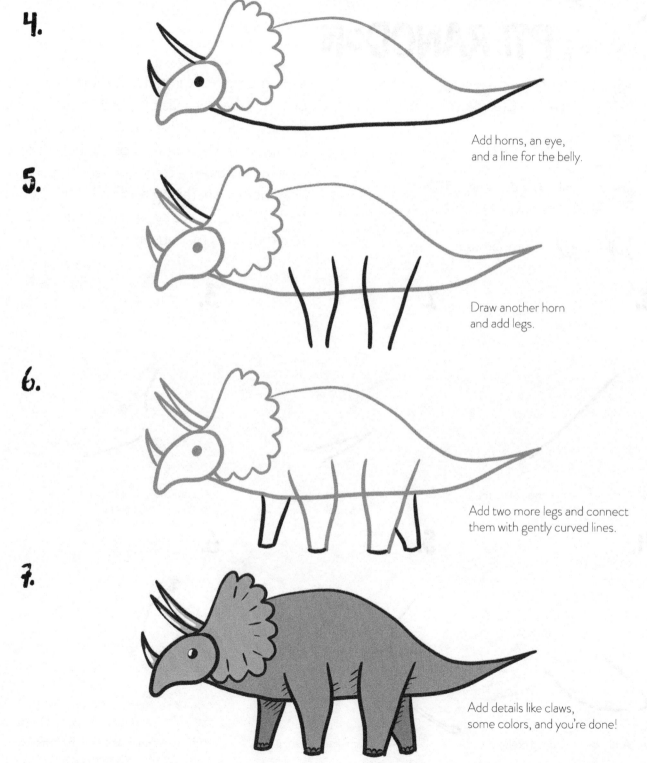

Add horns, an eye, and a line for the belly.

5.

Draw another horn and add legs.

6.

Add two more legs and connect them with gently curved lines.

7.

Add details like claws, some colors, and you're done!

11

PTERANODON

WHEN?		100-70 million years ago - in the Late Cretaceous period.
WEIGHT		20-50 pounds.
SIZE		Hight: 6 feet; Lenght: 10 feet; Wingspan up to 24 feet.
FOOD		Carnivorous.

Its name means winged and toothless. It flew over the shallow seas of North America. It was a flying reptile that lived during the time of the dinosaurs. It was not a dinosaur, but a close relative. It was able to glide over the ocean in large flocks, searching for fish in shallow water. Its crest could have served to attract a mate or as a rudder to maneuver in flight.

1.

Draw a diagonal line – this will be the front of the beak and forehead.

2.

Add an upside-down „v" – the beak.

3.

Draw the line of the lower beak, the back of the head, and a large eye.

4.

Add a bean-shaped body.

5.

Draw the arm line and a leg.

6.

Add a second, parallel line to complete the arm. Draw the claws .

12

7.

Draw two curved lines for the wings.

8.

Add two more curved lines for the wings. Add the second arm.

9.

Color in the Pteranodon, and it's ready to fly!

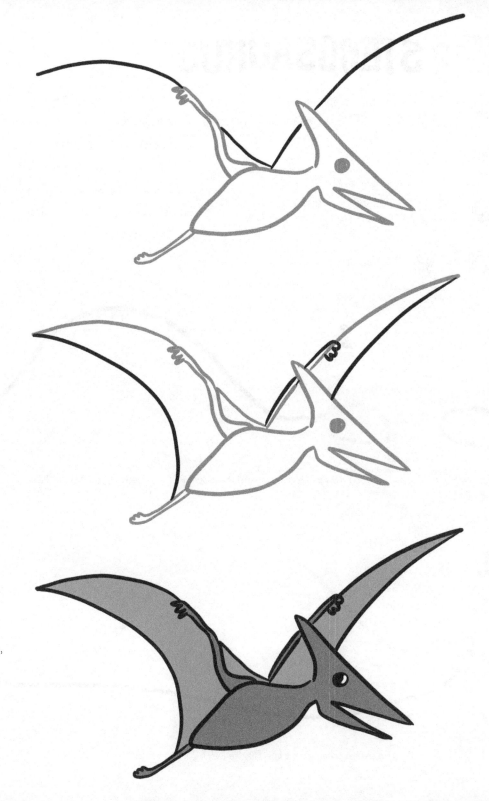

13

STEGOSAURUS

WHEN?		150 million years ago in the Late Jurassic/Early Cretaceous period.
WEIGHT		15,000 pounds.
SIZE		Height: 10 feet; Lenght: 30 feet; Plates: 2 feet; Tail spikes: 2-3 feet.
FOOD		Herbivorous.

It is one of the most iconic and easily recognizable dinosaurs of the Jurassic period. This giant herbivore is famous for its distinctive diamond-shaped plates and long spikes on its tail. These plates may have helped Stegosaurus regulate its body temperature or even protect it from predators!

1.

Start with a small head.

2.

Draw a long, rising, and then descending line for the back and tail.

3.

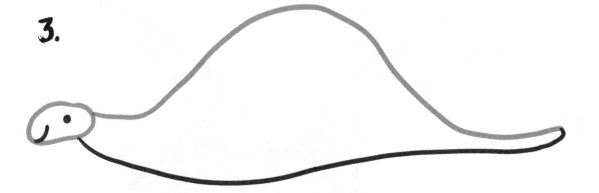

Add an eye, a smile, and a line for the belly.

4.

Draw four legs and sharp, triangular spikes on the head and neck.

5.

Close the legs at the bottom with gently curved lines. Add the characteristic square-ish plates on the back.

6.

Add necessary details, some colors, and you're done!

15

BRACHIOSAURUS

 154-150 million years ago - in the Late Jurassic period.

 Up to 128,000 pounds.

 Height: 50 feet; Lenght: 85 feet; Neck lenght up to 30 feet.

  Herbivorous.

Its name means arm lizard and refers to its deep thorax. It was one of the tallest and largest dinosaurs. With its huge front legs and very long neck, it could feed higher than most other dinosaurs. It had a large skull from which a large bulge stood out. This characteristic bony bar in the middle of the forehead served to separate the two nostrils.

1.

Start with a C shape - this will be the head.

2.

Next, draw a long neck, an eye, and a smile.

3.

Add a second curved line to complete the neck and another for the back and rear leg.

4.

Draw the front leg, rear leg, and tail.

5.

Add a curved line for the belly
and finish the tail.

6.

Draw the second front leg.

7.

Complete the legs and close them with gently
curved lines at the bottom.

8.

Finish with details like claws,
add some color, and you're done!

17

VELOCIRAPTOR

WHEN?
 75-71 million years ago-
in the late Cretaceous period.

WEIGHT
 33 pounds

SIZE
 Height: 1.6 feet; Lenght: 7 feet.

FOOD
🍽 🥩 Carnivorous.

Its name means "fast thief". The Velociraptor was actually smaller than how it is shown in movies and books, but it was still a speedy and scary hunter. The bumps on its arm bones show that it had feathers. It was likely warm-blooded, which means it could stay warm even in cooler weather, and it might have had soft fur to help keep it cozy and give it energy for hunting.

1.

Draw an elongated semicircle – this will be the back of the dinosaur's skull.

2.

Add a curved line – the upper jaw.

3.

Draw the lower jaw.

4.

Create an upside-down „S" shape – this will represent the back and tail.

5.
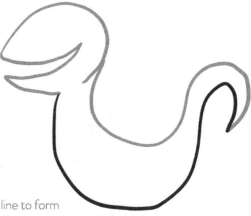

Draw a parallel line to form the torso and tail.

6.

Using broken lines, draw the upper and lower limbs. Add a nostril and an eye.

7.

Add additional limbs and claws. Draw a line separating the light-colored belly from the darker back.

8.

Add teeth and color in the dinosaur. Done!

SPINOSAURUS

WHEN? 95 million years ago - in the middle Cretaceous period.

WEIGHT 20,000 pounds.

SIZE Height: 20 feet; Lenght: 60 feet; Sail height: 5-6 feet.

FOOD Carnivorous. Fish and maybe other dinosaurs.

The Spinosaurus was a carnivorous dinosaur with enormous teeth and powerful jaws. This predator walked on two muscular legs and was relatively fast, allowing it to hunt both on land and in water. With its length and weight, it is considered one of the largest theropods.

1.

Start with a gently wavy, downward-sloping line for the jaw, head, back, and tail.

2.

Add a curved line wrapping around at the end to form the lower jaw.

3.

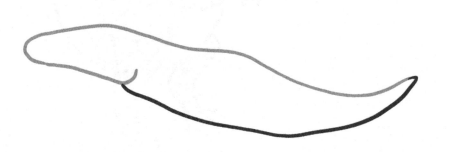

Draw a curved line for the belly.

4.

Draw the front
and hind masive legs.

5.

Add the line for the mouth,
an eye, and the sail on the back.

6.

Add details like sharp teeth, lines
on the sail, some color, a sparkle
in the eye, and you're done!

21

ANKYLOSAURUS

WHEN?		68-66 million years ago – in the late Cretaceous period.
WEIGHT		15,000 pounds.
SIZE		Height: 5.5 feet; Lenght: 26 feet; Tail club: 3 feet.
DIET		Herbivorous. Plant material, including ferns, shrubs and fruit.

Its name means armored reptile. It was well protected and well armed. Its thick skin was studded with hundreds of bony plates of different sizes, and its powerful tail mace could strike hard enough to shatter bones. Brain cavity analysis indicates that the most developed part of its brain was dedicated to its sense of smell.

1.

Draw a C shape and two cones – this will be the head and horns.

2.

Close the head with a V shape at the bottom.

3.

Draw a rounded line for the back and tail.

4.

Add a rounded line for the belly.

5.

Draw the eye, mouth, nostril, the massive legs, and the tail club.

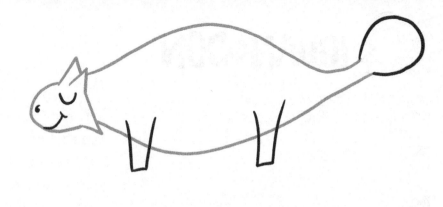

6.

Add the remaining legs, a line for the belly, and start drawing the plates on the body.

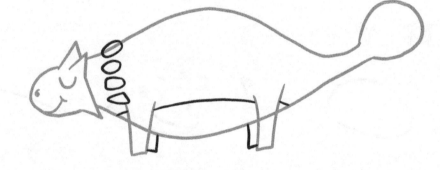

7.

Add more armor plates and claws.

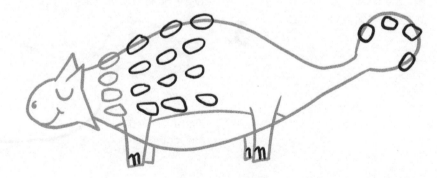

8.

Draw plates along the entire back and tail, add color, and you're done!

23

IGUANODON

WHEN?		140-110 million years ago – in the early Cretaceous period.
WEIGHT		10,000 pounds.
SIZE		Height: 10 feet; Lenght: 33 feet;
DIET		Herbivorous.

Its name means iguana tooth. It is an intermediate dinosaur, halfway between bipedal and fast dinosaurs and duck-billed dinosaurs. It was a grazing dinosaur that normally moved on four legs but could run on two. It had four fingers and a thumb equipped with a very sharp spur (3-6 inches) which it used to defend itself against predators.

1.

Draw an elongated, partially closed oval – this will be the head.

2.

Add the mouth line, nostril, and eye. Draw the line for the back and tail.

3.

Add a rounded line for the belly.

4.

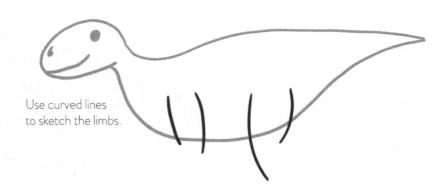

Use curved lines to sketch the limbs.

5. Continue drawing the limbs with additional arched lines.

6. Draw the feet and hands. Use semicircles to add the back plates.

7. Draw the fingers, thumb spike, and claws on the lower legs.

8. Add some color, and you're done!

25

DIPLODOCUS

WHEN?	155-145 million years ago – in the Late Jurassic period.
WEIGHT	30,000 pounds.
SIZE	Height: 15 feet tall at the hips. Lenght: 100 feet; neck: 26 feet; tail: 45 feet.
FOOD	Herbivorous. Leaves from trees and soft plants

Diplodocus was a long-necked herbivore known for its lightweight yet lengthy body. It had peg-like teeth suited for stripping leaves from tall trees and a long, whip-like tail that could have been used for defense or communication. Diplodocus is one of the best-known sauropods and is frequently featured in museums due to its enormous skeleton.

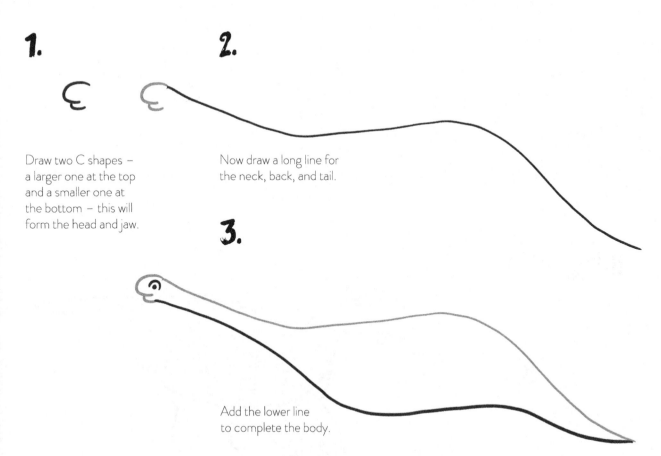

1.

Draw two C shapes – a larger one at the top and a smaller one at the bottom – this will form the head and jaw.

2.

Now draw a long line for the neck, back, and tail.

3.

Add the lower line to complete the body.

4.

Sketch massive legs.

5.

Close the legs and draw the additional ones.

6.

Draw a line separating the lighter underbelly from the darker upper body. Add claws.

7.

Color in the dinosaur, and you can add spikes on the back, neck, and tail. Done!

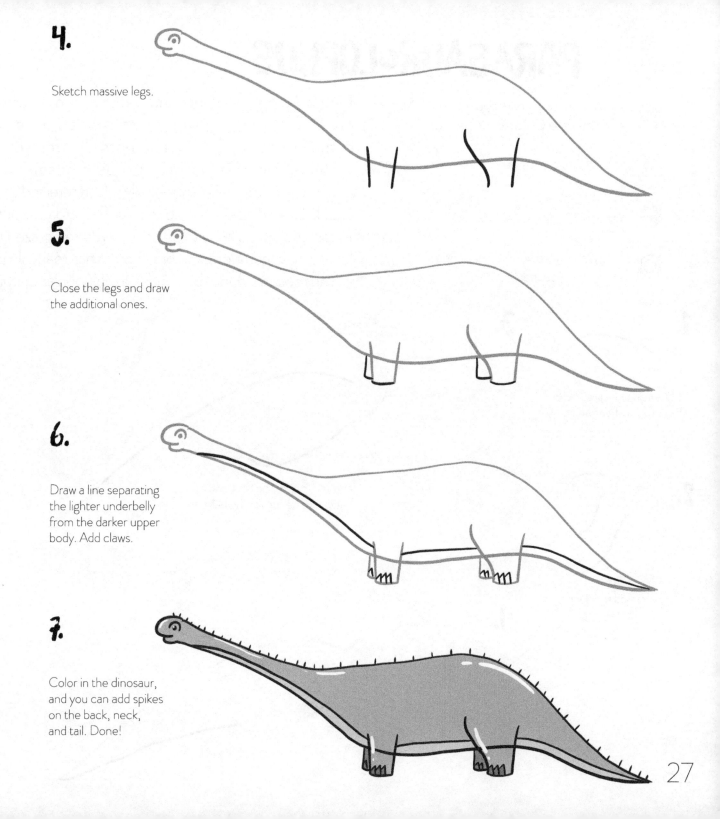

PARASAUROLOPHUS

WHEN?

77-73 million years ago - in the Late Cretaceous period.

WEIGHT

5,000 pounds.

SIZE

Hight: 10 feet; Lenght: 40 feet.

DIET

Herbivorous. Pine needles, tree leaves.

Parasaurolophus is best known for its long, curved crest, which is believed to have been used for communication, display, and possibly even sound amplification. This herbivorous dinosaur was a member of the hadrosaur family, often referred to as „duck-billed dinosaurs" due to their flat, broad snouts. Parasaurolophus likely traveled in herds and grazed on low-lying vegetation. Its unique crest has made it one of the most recognizable dinosaurs in popular culture.

1.

Draw an elongated bean shape for the head and crest.

2.

Add the neck.

3.

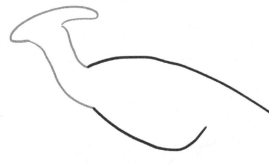

Draw the line for the back and tail, and add the line for the belly.

4.

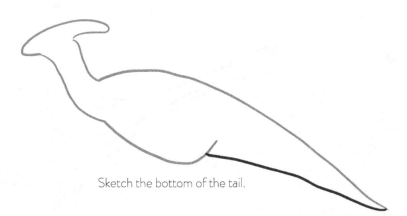

Sketch the bottom of the tail.

5.

Draw a narrow, long S shape –
this will be the strong hind leg.

6.

Add an eye. Complete the hind
leg, add a second leg, and draw
short front arms.

7.

Draw fingered claws.

8.

Color the top of the
dinosaur with a darker color.
Done!

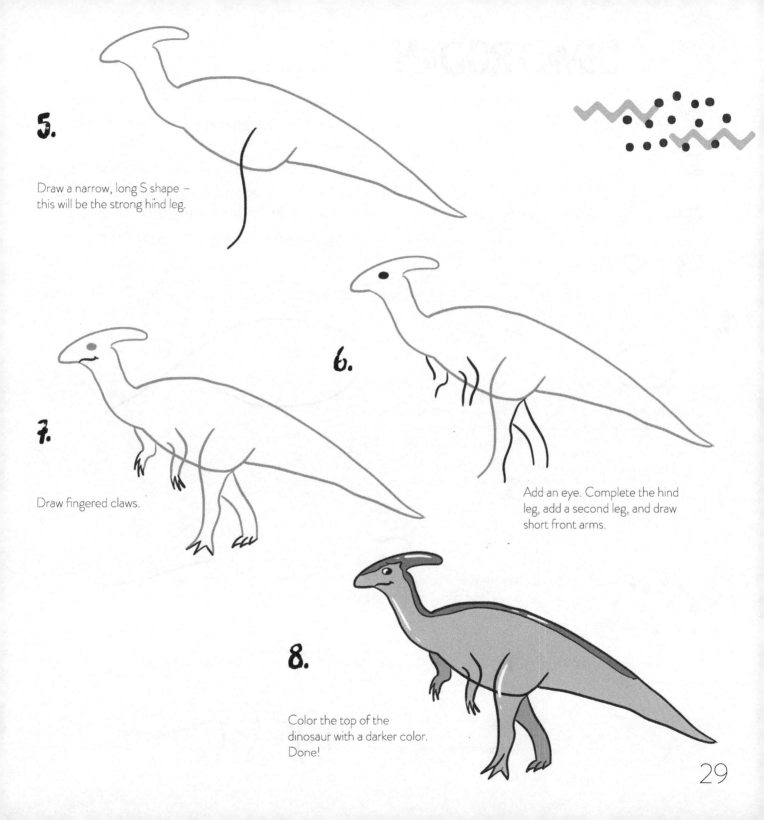

DIMETRODON

WHEN?		About 295 million years ago - in the Early Perm period.
WEIGHT		550 pounds.
SIZE		Height: 5 feet Lenght: 10 feet.
DIET		Carnivorous.

Although not a dinosaur, this prehistoric predator lived long before the first dinosaurs appeared. Its most distinctive feature was a large sail on its back, likely used to regulate body temperature. Dimetrodon had sharp teeth like a knife and walked on four legs, making it a strong hunter during its time.

1.

Start with an elongated C-shape – this will be the head.

2.

Draw two arched lines – one on top and one on the bottom to form the body and tail.

3.

Add the bottom of the tail. Draw large eyes, nostrils, and a smile.

4.

Add arcs for the legs.

5.

Draw lines extending upward from the back to outline the sail. Add claws.

6.

Connect the sail lines with curved arcs. Draw pupils and the remaining legs.

7.

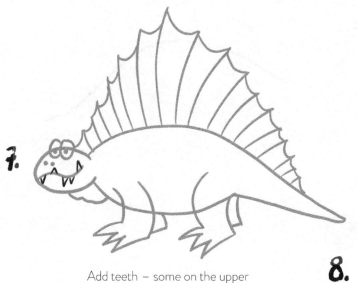

Add teeth – some on the upper and some on the lower jaw.

8.

Color the creature, and you can add spots on the body and a chin. Done!

PLESIOSAURUS

WHEN?	203-82 million years ago - Late Triassic to Late Cretaceous period.	
WEIGHT	2,000 pounds.	
SIZE	Lenght: 15 feet; neck lenght: 6 feet.	
DIET	Carnivorous.	

Plesiosaurus was a marine reptile, not a dinosaur, known for its long neck, small head, and broad, flat body with four flippers. It was well-adapted for swimming in the seas, using its paddle-like limbs to maneuver through the water. It is often depicted as an iconic sea creature of the Mesozoic Era.

1.

Start with an elongated
C-shape – this will be the head.

2.

Draw the eye, the mouth,
and the long neck.

3.

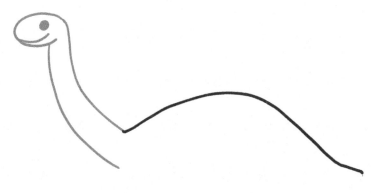

Add a curved line for the back.

4.

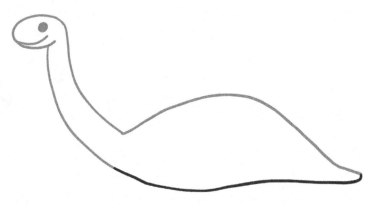

Sketch the line for the belly.

5.

Draw two vertical arcs for the
front flippers.

6.

Complete the flippers.

7.

Add the flippers on the opposite
side of the body.

8.

Color the creature. Done!

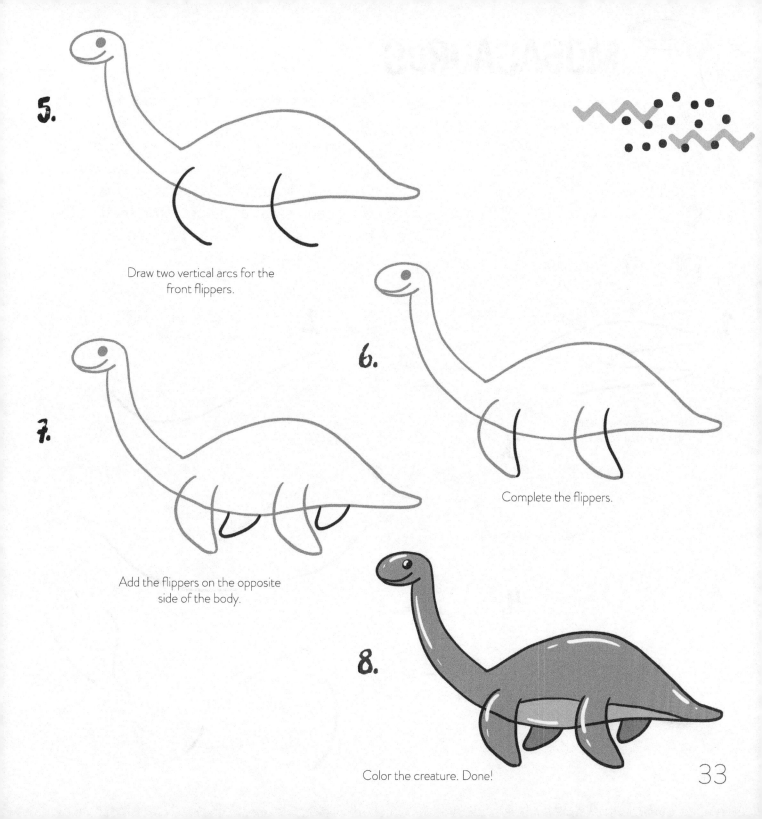

MOSASAURUS

WHEN?		82-66 million years ago - in the Late Cretaceous preiod.
WEIGHT		Up to 30,000 pounds.
SIZE		Lenght: 50 feet.
DIET		Carnivorous.

This giant marine reptile had a second set of teeth on the roof of its mouth, which helped it grip slippery prey more effectively. It had a long, streamlined body with powerful, paddle-like limbs and a large tail for swimming. Mosasaurus was a top predator, feeding on fish, sharks, and even other marine reptiles in the ancient seas.

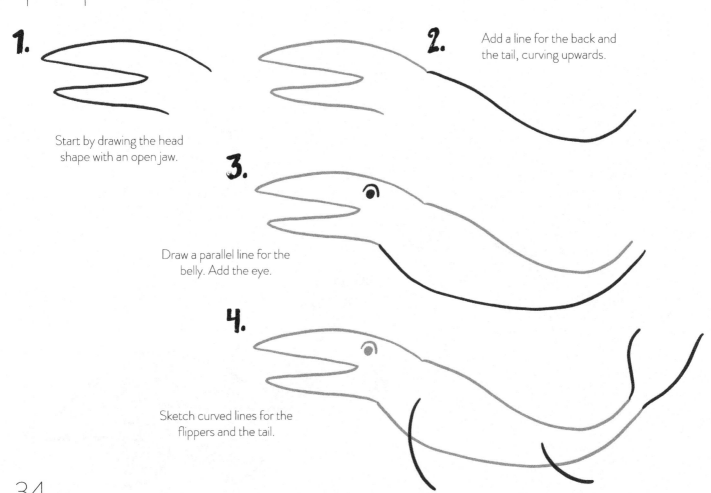

1. Start by drawing the head shape with an open jaw.

2. Add a line for the back and the tail, curving upwards.

3. Draw a parallel line for the belly. Add the eye.

4. Sketch curved lines for the flippers and the tail.

5.

Complete the flippers and tail with curved lines in the opposite direction.

6.

Add a line from the corner of the mouth to the tail.

7.

Draw large, sharp teeth, three parallel lines on the neck for the gills, and spikes on the back.

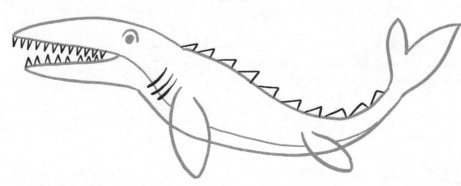

8.

Add some color, and you're done!

THERIZINOSAURUS

WHEN?		70-66 million years ago - in the Late Cretaceous preiod.
WEIGHT		11,000 pounds.
SIZE		Height: 20 feet; Lenght: 33 feet; Claw lenght: up to 3 feet.
DIET		Herbivorous.

This unusual dinosaur had enormous claws on its hands, reaching up to 3 feet in length, the longest of any known land animal. It had a bulky body, a long neck, and walked on two legs. Despite its fearsome appearance, Therizinosaurus is believed to have been an herbivore, using its claws to pull down branches and vegetation.

1.

Start with the top of the head – a semicircle and the line for the upper jaw.

2.

Add the eye, nostril, and the lower jaw.

3.

Draw the neck.

4.

Sketch two lines forming a bean - shaped body.

5.

Draw a tapering tail.

6.

Draw two C-shaped lines for the hind legs, and add one front arm.

7.

Complete the hind legs by drawing an elongated „3" shape. Draw the second front arm.

8.

Add the feet and long, sharp claws on the front arms.

9.

Draw the remaining claws and add claws to the hind legs.

10.

Color the dinosaur. Done!

37

CARNOTAURUS

WHEN?		71-69 million years ago - in the Late Cretaceous period.
WEIGHT		4,500 pounds.
SIZE		Height: 10 feet; Lenght: 30 feet.
DIET		Carnivorous.

Carnotaurus is one of the most peculiar and fascinating dinosaurs ever discovered. Its name means „meat-eating bull" because of the two cool horns above its eyes, which resemble those of a bull. These horns made Carnotaurus stand out from other dinosaurs. Another unique feature of this dinosaur was its tiny arms, which were even shorter than those of a T-Rex, making them some of the smallest arms of any known dinosaur!

1.

Start by drawing the head shape with an open jaw.

2.

Add the horns on top of the head.

3.

Draw the eye and nostril. Below the horns, add a curved line to create a 3D effect for the horns.

4.

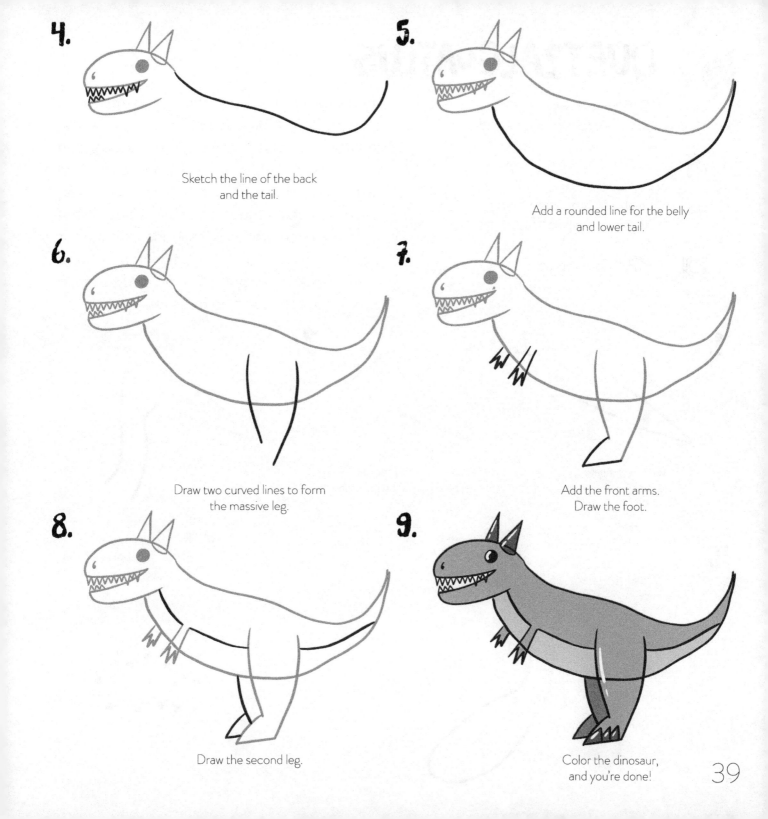

Sketch the line of the back
and the tail.

5.

Add a rounded line for the belly
and lower tail.

6.

Draw two curved lines to form
the massive leg.

7.

Add the front arms.
Draw the foot.

8.

Draw the second leg.

9.

Color the dinosaur,
and you're done!

QUETZALCOATLUS

WHEN? 70-66 million years ago - in the Late Cretaceous period.

WEIGHT 550 pounds.

SIZE Height: 16 feet; Lenght: 18 feet; Wingspan: up to 36 feet.

DIET Carnivorous.

Its name comes from the Aztec feathered serpent god, Quetzalcoatl. It was the largest flying animal that ever lived. It had a wingspan greater than that of a small plane and stood as tall as a giraffe. Despite its monstrous size, it did not weigh much and that is due to the complex system of air sacs inside its bones. It began its flight with a powerful jump of more than 10 feet in height and managed to reach a maximum speed of 55 miles per hour.

1.

Start with an elongated, pointed shape for the beak.

2.

Add another pointed shape on top — this will be the crest on its forehead.

3.

Draw a slightly curved neck.

4.

Create a small bean - -shaped body.

5.

Now for the wings: even though the shape seems complicated, you can draw it as a blocky spiral.

6.

Continue drawing the first wing. Then, add the second wing.

7.

Finish the wings and draw a leg.

8.

Add spikes on the wings and complete the legs.

9.

Add some details to the head, and draw the eye.

10.

Color the dinosaur, and you're done!

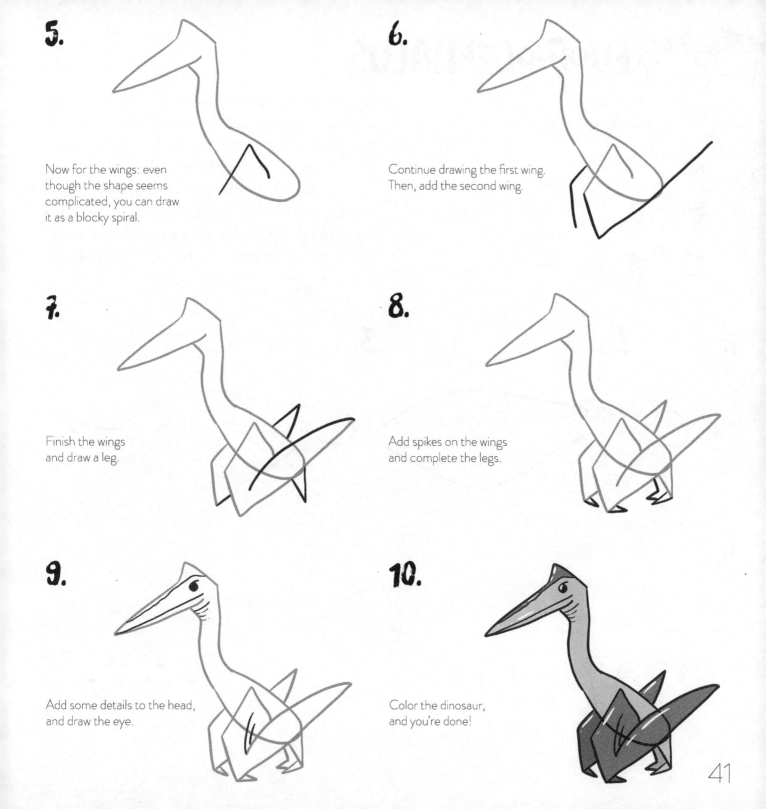

41

 # EUOPLOCEPHALUS

WHEN?		76-70 million years ago - in the Late Cretaceous period.
WEIGHT		5,000 pounds.
SIZE		Height: 5 feet; Lenght: 25 feet; Width: 10 feet.
DIET		Herbivorous.

Its name means well armored head. It is one of the most studied and best represented dinosaurs. It stood out for its exceptional armor, which provided the best defense against predators. They rarely approached, and if they did, it would defend itself by turning to the side and striking with its tail. However, it had a weak point: if a predator overturned the animal, it would become defenseless.

1.

2.

3.

Start with a C-shaped head.

Draw an elongated body.

Add a tapering tail.

4.

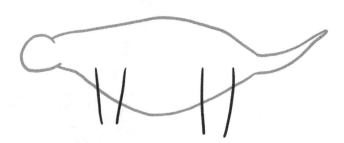

Sketch massive legs.

42

5.

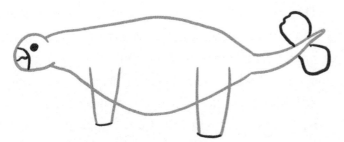

Draw the snout and eye. Close
the bottom of the legs. Add two
spheres at the end of the tail.

6.

Begin drawing the armor plates.

7.

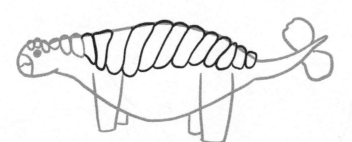

Continue adding more armor plates.

8.

Draw spikes on the back.

9.

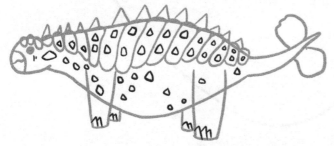

Add more spikes all over the body and draw claws.

10.

Color the dinosaur, and you're done!

43

COMPSOGNATHUS

WHEN?		161-146 million years ago - in the Late Jurassic period.
WEIGHT		10 pounds.
SIZE		Height: 2 feet; Lenght: 3-4 feet.
DIET		Omnivores.

This dinosaur had a unique feature: it is one of the few dinosaurs whose fossilized stomach contents have been found, giving scientists rare insights into its last meal. It had a lightweight, bird-like skeleton, and its long tail helped it maintain balance while running at high speeds. Compsognathus was one of the smallest known dinosaurs.

1.

Start by drawing the head shape with an open jaw.

2.

Next, draw a downward curved arc for the back and tail.

3.

Draw a parallel line for the belly.

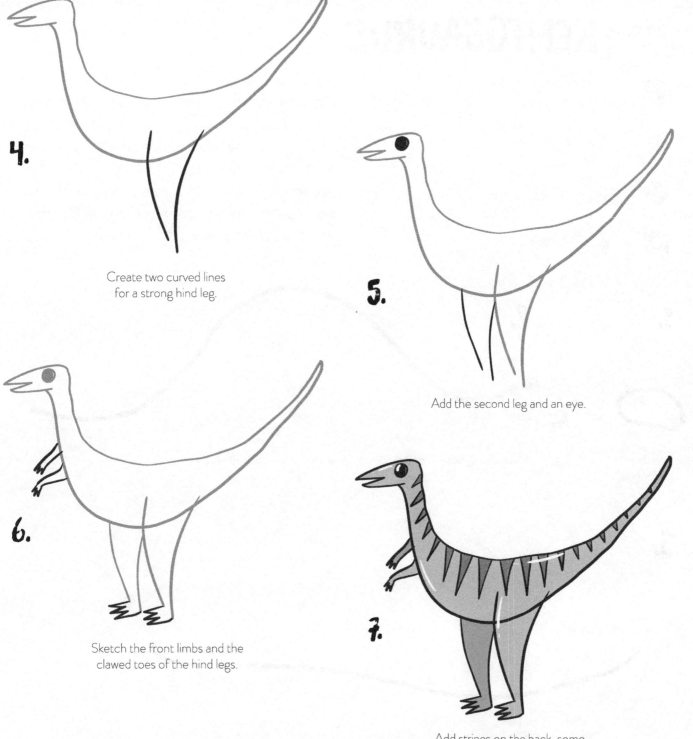

4. Create two curved lines for a strong hind leg.

5. Add the second leg and an eye.

6. Sketch the front limbs and the clawed toes of the hind legs.

7. Add stripes on the back, some color, and you're done!

KENTOSAURUS

WHEN? 150 million years ago in the Late Jurassic/Early Cretaceous period.

WEIGHT 2,500 pounds.

SIZE Height: 8 feet; Lenght: 20 feet.

FOOD   Herbivorous.

Kentrosaurus stood out due to its unique combination of defensive armor. It had rows of sharp spikes running along its back and tail, with particularly long and intimidating spikes on its hips. These spikes not only provided protection from predators but may have also been used during competition with other members of its species.

1.

Start with a small head.

2.

Draw a long, rising, and then descending line for the back and tail.

3.

Add an eye, a smile, and a line for the belly.

4.

Draw four legs and sharp, triangular spikes on the head and neck.

5.

Close the legs at the bottom with gently curved lines. Add the characteristic square-ish plates and spikes along its back and tail.

6.

Add necessary details, some colors, and you're done!

STYGIMOLOCH

WHEN?		Around 66 million years ago - in the Late Cretaceous period.
WEIGHT		200 pounds.
SIZE		Height: 8 feet; Lenght: 12 feet.
FOOD		Herbivorous.

Stygimoloch was like a dinosaur with a cool helmet on its head! It had a bumpy, dome-shaped skull covered in spikes. Scientists think it might have used its head to bump into other Stygimolochs, kind of like how some animals play today!

1.

Draw an oval shape for the head. Add an eye.

2.

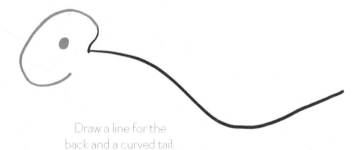

Draw a line for the back and a curved tail.

3.

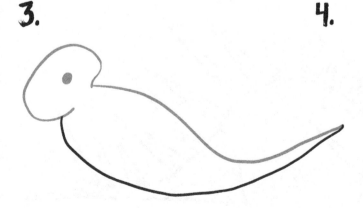

Sketch a curved line for the belly and the bottom of the tail.

4.

Draw a line on the top of the head to create the skull armor. Then, draw the legs.

5.

Add two more curved lines for the hind legs. Draw the arms.

6.

Draw the snout, along with spikes and horns on the skull. Add clawed feet.

7.

Add more spikes and horns. Sketch stripes on the back.

8.

Color the dinosaur, and you're done!

T-REX SKELETON

The skeleton of Tyrannosaurus Rex is one of the most fascinating discoveries in paleontology. A full-grown T-Rex had around 200 bones, and its skull alone could be as long as 5 feet! The T. Rex had an incredibly strong, thick skull, designed to support its powerful jaws. Interestingly, its tiny arms had just two fingers and were much smaller in proportion to its massive body, possibly helping with balance. Despite the small arms, its powerful legs and large, strong bones suggest it was an efficient predator.

1.  Start with a light sketch of the dinosaur – this will be our base. We'll draw the bones inside.

2.  Draw the skull.

3.  Add the eye socket. Draw the jawline with teeth. Below the head, sketch oval shapes – these will be the cervical vertebrae.

4. 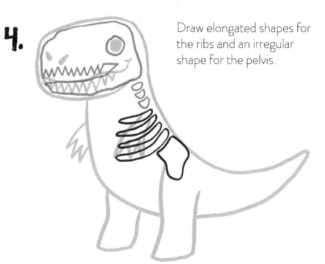 Draw elongated shapes for the ribs and an irregular shape for the pelvis.

5. Sketch the limbs and the tail.

6. Draw bean-shaped forms for the bones of the limbs, ending with the phalanges. Add cross-sections for the tail vertebrae.

7.

8.

The skeleton should be white, so color the background dark, leaving the bones white, like the paper. Of course, you can also color the skeleton if you wish!

STEGOSAURUS SKELETON

The skeleton of Stegosaurus is unique and easily recognizable. This dinosaur had 17 large, bony plates along its back, supported by its vertebrae, and four sharp tail spikes, called the thagomizer, used for defense. Its skull was small compared to its body, which could be up to 30 feet long, and it had short, robust legs. Despite its massive body, Stegosaurus had one of the smallest brains for its size, around the size of a walnut, indicating it wasn't very intelligent but well-adapted for survival!

1.

Start with a light sketch of the dinosaur – this will be our base. We'll draw the bones inside.

2.

Draw the skull. Add the eye socket. Draw the jawline with teeth. Sketch oval shapes – these will be the cervical vertebrae.

3.

Draw elongated shapes for the ribs and an irregular shape for the pelvis.

4.

Draw the spikes on the head and neck. Add the bones of the legs and the vertebrae of the tail.

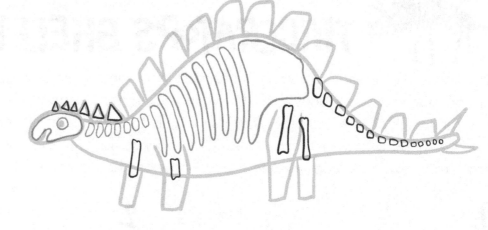

5.

Sketch the bones of the limbs, completing the skeleton. Draw the characteristic squarish plates and spikes on the back and tail.

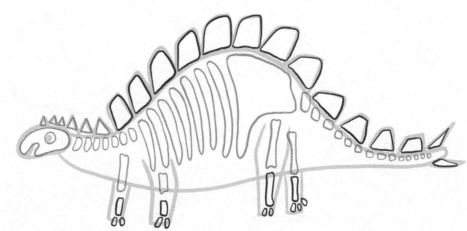

6.

The skeleton should be white, so color the background dark, leaving the bones white, like the paper. Of course, you can also color the skeleton if you wish!

TRICERATOPS SKELETON

The skeleton of Triceratops is one of the most iconic among dinosaurs. Its massive skull featured three distinct horns: two long ones above its eyes and a shorter one on the nose. The large bony frill extended from the back of its head, protecting its neck. Triceratops had a strong, stocky body with four sturdy legs, to support its weight of up to 26,000 pounds. Its beak-like mouth and powerful jaw helped it crush tough plant material, making it a well-equipped herbivore in its environment.

1.

Start with a light sketch of the
dinosaur – this will be our base.
We'll draw the bones inside.

2.

Draw the characteristic skull.

3.

Draw the three horns
and the eye socket.

4.

Sketch the ribs.

5.

Draw the pelvis.

6.

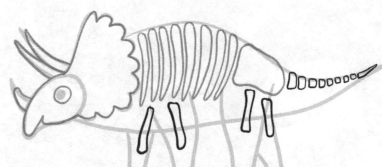

Add the upper limb bones and tail vertebrae.

7.

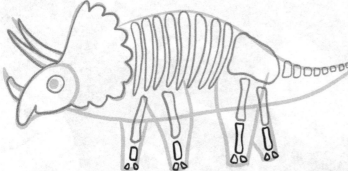

Draw the bones of the limbs.

The skeleton should be white, so color the background dark, leaving the bones white, like the paper. Of course, you can also color the skeleton if you wish!

8.

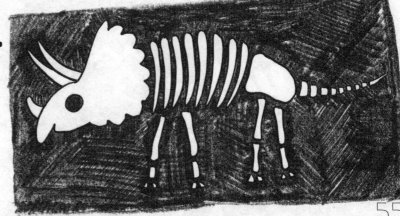

THANK YOU!

Dear parents, when creating this "How to Draw..." book series, our goal was to offer a tool that helps your children draw with ease, beginning from the most basic shapes. We believe that this approach will bring children immense joy as they watch dinosaurs come to life from simple circles, ovals and lines. If you find this book beneficial, please share your feedback, which could help others in making their choice. We wish you and your child many delightful moments of creativity and fun!

Made in the USA
Monee, IL
29 December 2024